HOW TO MAKE
SUCCESSFUL
APPOINTMENTS

WRITTEN BY
Tessa Scott-Thomas

PUBLISHED BY
Little Demon Publishing Company Limited
Droitwich
Worcestershire
WR9 OAJ
Telephone: + 44 0800 358 8003
Facsimile: + 44 (0) 1905 451221
E-Mail: publishing@littledemon.com

Published in Great Britain

EDITORS
Julie Hamilton, David Crewdson and Geoff Marsh.

TYPESETTING AND DESIGN
Creative Warehouse, Worcester.

PRINTING
Printed and bound in the UK

Introduction

Contacting people for appointments is regarded as one of the most difficult activities for sales and non-sales professionals alike. Even though it is considered a primary function of every sales organisation, and the only way to ensure career success, it is still the area most likely to cause problems.

" I really hate making appointments over the telephone"

Being able to make successful appointments is a vital requirement in business today. It is essential to arrange face-to-face meetings to ensure that your product or service has the best advantage in being promoted. Yet, without training, sales people will waste their time in a number of recognised ways, from simple call aversion (not picking up the telephone in the first place) to making an appointment with the wrong prospect.

"I avoid training courses - they are a waste of my valuable sales time"

Many people believe that their status as a sales person immediately puts them at a disadvantage in any confrontation. How many of you have been asked, "Are you selling something?" and quickly responded with a "No". It's difficult to be proud of your product or service if you're keeping it a secret! You have, after all, chosen to represent it by taking the job.

" I am an account manager, not a sales person"

If you believe that sales people are aggressive, persistent and annoying - people who won't take 'no' for an answer - then that is probably how you view yourself when you are trying to make telephone appointments. Attempting to change this image by enhancing job titles from sales representative to consultant or adviser, sends a clear message that sales is a dirty word - so acting in any way like the old stereotype will cause you problems.

Sales is a fantastic profession. It can be fun, financially rewarding and, unlike most other jobs, offers lots of personal freedom.

By putting our hot tips and ideas into practice, making those appointments will be a lot easier and prove to be more financially rewarding. Start on your pathway to success by overcoming your own demons today!

Sales demon

" I am a hard working **SALES DEMON.** *I am here to help you succeed. I'll point out any smart ideas and red hot tips to keep you motivated and achieve excellent results.*"

POSITIVE DEMON

"*I am a* **LAZY DEMON.** *I don't care if you fail. The less time you spend selling, the greater satisfaction I get. I'll make sure your sales performance is always poor so you'll never have a high income. I feed on your failure.*"

NEGATIVE DEMON

Contents

Sales aversion

- ☐ Butterflies in the stomach
- ☐ Excessive perspiration
- ☐ Heart pounding
- ☐ Excessive movement - fidgeting
- ☐ Breathing faster
- ☐ Incessant talking
- ☐ Chest feels tight

- ☐ Need to visit the bathroom more often
- ☐ Voice raising to a higher pitch
- ☐ Mind going blank
- ☐ Shaking hands
- ☐ Stammering and stuttering

Recognise any of these?

These are the sensations the negative demons just love. Try to come to terms with these feelings uses up a lot of valuable sales energy.

"MY FAVOURITE - *the one you waste most time on, and this gives me the greatest pleasure."*

"This is **YOUR** *fear driven by your reluctance to make that telephone call. Everyone experiences it at some time or other. I show you ways to keep your negative demons hungry. The satisfaction of success will then be yours, read on."*

2

Sales aversion
THE NEGATIVE DEMON'S PARADISE

The sales aversion demon is there to distract you and diverts your energy to help you fail. This demon has one purpose - to make you feel so fearful about contacting people that you'd do anything else rather than pick up the telephone and start to make appointments.

"I'll call later . . . this is a busy time . . . everyone will be at lunch . . . I'll wait until they receive the mailing"

Being fearful about calling a customer for an appointment can be almost as terrifying as facing a charging elephant. In these situations you experience sensations linked to a response called 'fight or flight'. A strong rush of adrenaline can be felt stimulating muscles to prepare for action and the need to protect oneself by either fighting or running away. Making a telephone call may not be as dangerous as facing a wild animal, but your instincts will react in the same way. If you are experiencing these sensations, strongly and on a regular basis, you will subconsciously be managing the emotional behaviour to calm the adrenaline rush. This drain of energy has a negative impact on your ability to make contact with people and gain appointments.

I am not reluctant to call anyone after all.....

"I use the telephone everyday to order pizza - book restaurants - ask people out for dates"

It seems a lot of sales people can be experts in the wrong field - like how to avoid making the sales calls. This avoidance is triggered by the need to alleviate the fears and calm the body down. But those nagging sensations are not going to go away. The only way open to the negative salesman is to channel this excess energy into pacing around aimlessly, checking the car, organising and then re-organising customer record cards, paying an extended visit to the bathroom or chatting for hours on end at the coffee machine!

Take control of your future success - reclaim your energy from negative behaviour and beat your demons

Sales aversion
THE NEGATIVE DEMON'S PARADISE

It is a positive way of avoiding what is felt as the cause, i.e. calling for that appointment. Don't let your imagination fool you into preparing for negatives such as:

- **Cold unhelpful receptionists**
- **Aggressive customers with no time**
- **Sounding stupid by forgetting the sales script**
- **Colleagues are listening**
- **Being told 'not interested'**

If you identify with this, then your common sense should tell you that by making the call you are more likely to succeed than to fail. Most people enjoy an opportunity to buy and your call could be just what they were waiting for. Call the sales department of your target company and see how they react to a fellow sales person. They might even be able to help you and will certainly respect your professional sales attitude.

When you recognise and overcome your own negative demon that feeds on sales aversion you will remove some of your biggest barriers to success.

"*I used to shut myself away in an office, shuffle my record cards, dial the number, let it ring a few times and put the phone down if someone walked into the room so that I wouldn't be overheard. Now I realise that there are golden nuggets at the end of each phone call, all capable of increasing my chances of success.*
Effort always pays off." - YUK!

Now focus and dial that number.

Sales aversion
REMEMBER

"ALWAYS USE THE TIME AFTER YOU'VE MADE A SUCCESSFUL CALL TO MAKE ANOTHER CALL.

You'll be more confident (which will reflect in your voice) and you'll be more motivated to succeed.

"MAKE EVERY CONTACT WITH SOMEONE COUNT.

Use the techniques we will give you and make contacting customers a positive experience to help you and your business."

How to make a successful appointment in 10 easy stages

Here are easy steps to follow, which we will cover in more detail along the way:

1 **Use The Demon Sales Cycle**

2 **Prepare your own words**

3 **Research your customer details and prepare high quality leads**

4 **Identify your potential buyers**

5 **Making the call - use energy to get appointments**

6 **Use your sales skills to arouse interest - probe for information, introduce features, advantages and benefits**

7 **Use your sales skills to overcome objections and to listen**

8 **Ask for the meeting and be prepared to offer alternative dates or times**

9 **Closing the call**

10 **Confirm the appointment then update your records and database**

How to make a successful appointment in 10 easy stages
1. DEMON SALES CYCLE

This is our wicked sales cycle - a set of activities which need to happen in order to secure business from potential customers.

Each element of the sales cycle can be considered a point of entry at anytime. For example, let's assume you are part of an implementation team for a large computer company who've already sold their products into a company. This need not be the end of the sales process. During your 'aftersales' call, you can ask for a referral to another organisation that might benefit from your product. Information from your existing happy customer has now started the 'research, preparation and planning' stage of a new sales process. The cycle is continuous so, no matter where you come in, you'll be setting in motion another potentially successful sales cycle.

How to make a successful appointment in 10 easy stages
1. GATEKEEPER NEGATIVE DEMON

How many times have you answered the phone, to hear a sharp intake of breath and a familiar sales monotone such as, "If you could change any window in your house, which one would you start with?" or, "We are conducting a survey, do you have two minutes to answer some questions?" Why do they always ring when you've just sat down to watch your favourite television program or you've just got into a bath, and why do they sometimes get your name wrong? Think for a minute how you respond to such calls. Do you get angry? Are you polite? Or do you just put the phone down? Is this how you think your customers will react to your call?

Maybe the person who called sounded as if they weren't really interested in you (by getting your name wrong for a start!), or treated you as no more than a sales prospect. You may have come across this during your training.

Next time you have a sales call at home or at work, why not ask them for relevant details of their organisation? After all, they have called you and trading contact names could be of considerable benefit to both of you.

How to make a successful appointment in 10 easy stages

I. GATEKEEPER NEGATIVE DEMON

DO THEY STILL EXIST?

"The idea that having to employ clever tactics to actually get to the buyer has been a long held belief by some sales trainers.

In my experience and from the feedback I've received, the practice of gatekeepers is now as extinct as having two personal secretaries to guard one senior executive.

Many buyers can now be reached by e-mail and are quite accessible. Yes, I agree that there will always be some kind of reaction to overcome such as a receptionist asking the purpose of your call (a reasonable question since he/she has been briefed to ask this by an employer).

My advice is to be yourself and NOT learn the techniques in this book.

IT WILL ENSURE THAT YOU FAIL"

How to make a successful appointment in 10 easy stages
2. PREPARING YOUR OWN WORDS IS A GREAT SAFETY NET

Many large and successful organisations ensure a consistency of approach to calling customers for appointments by preparing a script. As many actors will tell you, when it comes to giving a successful performance, they have to start with a good script.

There are of course, the exceptional few who prefer to ad lib, but this is a special talent that takes years of practice. So why go to the trouble of writing your own words? The better prepared you are, the more relaxed you will feel when you start to make appointments (remember those negative sensations such as butterflies in the stomach, muddling up words, etc.).

Here are a few hot tips to help you put down the words that you'll feel comfortable using.

Remember that preparing your own words will act as a safety net for the first set of appointments that you make. The more calls you make, the more meetings you will arrange; the more your confidence builds, the less you will rely on your 'script'. There are very few things that you can do in business without preparation. Having your own words in front of you cuts confusion and is a great asset if you start to experience any negative sensations. If you forget what to say, just review where you are and carry on. You can always change a word or phrase until you feel comfortable with what you are saying. Run through it several times. Try practising with someone until you are relaxed with the responses that you need to give.

We have all been given at least one sales script which uses words we as individuals are uncomfortable with. The best solution is to rewrite your script, keeping to the basic principles but using words that suit your own unique style. Just as you will adapt the tips and ideas in this book to match your individual needs.

How to make a successful appointment in 10 easy stages

2. PREPARING YOUR OWN WORDS IS A GREAT SAFETY NET

"Write out the whole conversation that you intend to have, starting with,

'HELLO, MY NAME IS ...

The reason I am calling today is to find out who buys X for your company'.

Anticipate any questions the receptionist may ask you and be ready with a response (don't get tongue tied at this early stage).

Now anticipate the questions the customer may ask you. Put yourself in their shoes and ask yourself why you think the product/service will meet their needs."

How to make a successful appointment in 10 easy stages
3. RESEARCHING YOUR CUSTOMER DETAILS

Many successful sales professionals will tell you that the amount of research you do before making contact with customers will determine how successful you will be. The more information you have on the person and company you are contacting, the better prepared you are to present the benefits of your product or service. Many people are both surprised and flattered when talking with someone who is well informed about their organisation and the role they perform within it.

Finding leads is always a challenge but there are lots of simple ways to gain the information you need. Here are some obvious sources that are readily available.

- **Networking (local clubs, groups, internet)**
- **Trade directories and magazines**
- **Contacts supplied by existing customers (referrals)**
- **Exhibitions or trade shows**
- **Existing suppliers**
- **Business associations and institutes**
- **Corporate or internet databases**
- **Press - national, local, trade or technical**
- **Company brochures, annual reports and internal directories**
- **Small business associations**
- **Multiple stockists/buyers for your product**
- **Colleagues, friends and family**
- **Libraries/telephone directories**
- **'Orphan' client lists**

How to make a successful appointment in 10 easy stages

3. RESEARCHING YOUR CUSTOMER DETAILS

"PREPARE A FILE WITH DETAILS OF YOUR PROSPECTIVE CUSTOMERS.

Include any interesting facts, such as recent newspaper/magazine articles, stock market reports, recruitment adverts, etc. Gather as much information as you can.

This is detective work that will really pay off!

The more data and information that you collect, the better prepared you will be when you contact your customer for an appointment."

How to make a successful appointment in 10 easy stages

3. RESEARCHING YOUR CUSTOMER DETAILS

"Go through a paper's job section to get the names of staff and a telephone number you can contact!"

"Research is easy - look at the situations vacant section. Here is a good example."

Typical job advertisement.

DIRECTOR OF GLOBAL PERSONNEL RESOURCE
SALARY £ 90,000 + benefits

Our company has opened new offices in Honk Kong, Singapore, New York, London, Zurich, Amsterdam and Berlin. We are recruiting staff for all of these locations and require a Director to oversee the planned expansion of staff. We have a successful succession planning programme with minimal staff turnover.

JONES PLC
(SINCE 1889)

1234 High Street London ECU 777
Contact: Lynn Smith Title: Managing Director
Telephone:01234 56789 Fax: 01234 56789 E-mail: lynn@jonesplc.com

---

Questions:

- **Are they high payers?**
- **Are they expanding?**
- **How many years in business?**
- **Training, do they invest?**
- **Turnover per annum, high or low?**

How to make a successful appointment in 10 easy stages
3. PREPARING QUALITY 'HOT' LEADS

All sales leads are not necessarily of the right quality to produce results and can even be a source of irritation if you come to rely on them from other people. It is advisable therefore, to begin generating your own leads based on the research you have carried out and verified. If you are currently working with 'cold' leads you may have to use your system to enhance them to quality 'hot' leads. You will then start to build the information you need to make a successful appointment. Measure the quality of your leads by checking them against this list.

- **Customer address**
- **Telephone number (direct line if possible) or e-mail address**
- **Contact name**
- **Contact title**
- **Company background**
- **Relevant details (competitors, buying capacity, etc.).**
- **Grade - 'Hot', 'Warm' or 'Cold'**

To determine the quality of the leads, ensure all the above details are present. Gather as much information as possible about their purchasing plans, e.g. are they looking to buy now, next month or next year? Maybe they have been making specific sales enquiries or they are planning to expand. All of these points are very important and will assist you when grading each lead. The information will also help you to prioritise which customers should be contacted first.

Hot leads = Lots of contact has taken place. All details have been confirmed and are up to date.

Medium Leads = Contact has been made but some information is missing or out of date.

Cold Leads = No contact has taken place before. Details are suspect or out of date.

HOT LEADS MAKE MONEY

How to make a successful appointment in 10 easy stages
4. IDENTIFYING THE POTENTIAL BUYER

Research will determine whom, within the target organisation, might be a prospective buyer. A name alone will not be sufficient. Here are some questions that will need answering to ensure you have all the relevant information.

- **Who is the decision-maker for your particular product or service?**
- **What is their title/status within the organisation?**
- **Which department do they work in?**
- **What benefits of your product or service would they be most interested in?**
- **What are their usual payment terms?**
- **What is the financial status of the organisation?**
- **How long have they been in business?**
- **What is their preferred buying style?**
- **Who is their existing supplier and for how long?**
- **Have they ever bought from you in the past?**

Always make the appointment with the person with the:

MONEY
AUTHORITY
NEED
"Otherwise you'll be wasting your time."

(The only exception being if the person with whom you have the appointment has influence with the ultimate decision-maker).

How to make a successful appointment in 10 easy stages
5. MAKING THE CALL

"IF YOU COME ACROSS VOICEMAIL, LEAVE YOUR NAME AND TELEPHONE NUMBER ONLY"
(no company name).
This way, people usually return your call.

"ALWAYS FIND THE MD'S FIRST AND LAST NAMES.
Using his name when telling the receptionist that he asked you to call will get results!"

How to make a successful appointment in 10 easy stages
6. USING YOUR SALES SKILLS – AROUSING INTEREST

Remember that old sales hook - What's In It For Me? (W.I.I.F.M.)

It's human nature to adopt a 'What's In It For Me?' attitude. So majoring on the benefits your product or service will offer to the customer is vital if you are going to get their attention.

It's also going to ensure you are listened to with some interest. If a customer seems hesitant to commit to an appointment with you it may be because you have not considered the most important rule of human nature.

What's In It For Me?

Put yourself in their shoes for a moment and consider what benefits your product or service can offer them?

If for instance they've had difficulty with a previous supplier, what can you offer to ensure they have a trouble free alternative?

If they are trying to complete a difficult project - how can you help them to succeed? If they received bad advice from a sales person in the past, how can you win their trust and encourage them to buy from you?

Don't be afraid to ask effective open questions to find out about them (remember the negative demon when you pick up the phone to a cold caller). Are they currently involved with a promotion? Or merging with another company perhaps? Your research will give you some open questions to ask them. Build up a good rapport before finding the opportunity of introducing the benefits of your product or service to them.

How to make a successful appointment in 10 easy stages
6. USING YOUR SALES SKILLS - AROUSING INTEREST

"WRITE A W.I.I.F.M. FOR A POTENTIAL BUYER THAT YOU'VE RESEARCHED. *Get into the habit of doing this for all your potential customers.*

Do this as part of your preparation before you make the call.

It always works for me."

How to make a successful appointment in 10 easy stages
6. USING YOUR SALES SKILLS - PROBING FOR INFORMATION

The buyer is now listening to you, as you have aroused his/her interest. This is the stage in the sales cycle where you need to probe for valuable information and listen carefully to what is being said.

The buyer will be quite happy to answer your questions as long as they do not seem to be read from a script! So again, use your own words.

It is essential you get as much information as possible so that you can assess the customer's needs and match them with the benefits your product or service will offer. To move from a cold relationship, you first need to put at ease the person you are talking to by asking relevant questions (again, these should have been prepared at the research stage).

People love to talk about themselves. The most successful business people will tell you, "I listen for a living!" With practice you will soon be able to anticipate the next question you should be asking and tailor it to suit the response from the last. Trust your instincts, it's easy!

Open questions encourage a more informative response and leave little opportunity for one-word answers. This is a basic sales skill, but a skill that nevertheless needs to be honed to perfection to maximise your success levels.

Closed questions shut conversations down to one-word answers - what do you expect to learn from a customer's "yes" or "no" answer? Closed questions begin with do, will, if, can, did, etc. Avoid them.

How to make a successful appointment in 10 easy stages

6. USING YOUR SALES SKILLS - PROBING FOR INFORMATION

> *"Use the prefix:*
>
> ***WHO?***
>
> ***WHAT?***
>
> ***WHERE?***
>
> ***WHEN?***
>
> ***HOW?***
>
> *and **WHY?***
>
> *Prepare your open questions to confirm information you pick up during the call. This builds rapport by showing that you are paying interest. It usually helps to pose questions in the past tense rather than in the future. You will normally find that people are happy to answer questions about things that have happened and will usually give you reasonably factual replies."*

How to make a successful appointment in 10 easy stages

6. USING YOUR SALES SKILLS - INTRODUCING FEATURES, ADVANTAGES AND BENEFITS

How will your product or service satisfy a customer's requirements? Why should they buy from you?

Because the Features, Advantages and Benefits (F.A.B.'s) you offer are far superior to those of the competition.

These distinct advantages are called the Unique Selling Points (U.S.P.'s) and are present in every type of product or service on offer, e.g. Demon Sales Training offers practical tips and advice for busy sales professionals who want to learn how to achieve business targets using the most successful methods possible.

If you don't know the Features, Advantages and Benefits of your product or service it is essential you start to get to know them now. Otherwise, how do you expect to respond to enquiries, prepare a sales proposal or present and negotiate for new business?

Here are some comparison checks you should make before preparing your F.A.B.'s

- **What does the competition offer?**
- **What are their current costs and delivery times?**
- **What type of service do they sell?**
- **What are their Unique Selling Points (U.S.P.'s)?**
- **What are their F.A.B.'s?**
- **Why is your product or service better?**
- **What are your Unique Selling Points?**

How to make a successful appointment in 10 easy stages

6. USING YOUR SALES SKILLS - INTRODUCING FEATURES, ADVANTAGES AND BENEFITS

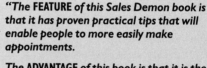

"The **FEATURE** of this Sales Demon book is that it has proven practical tips that will enable people to more easily make appointments.

The **ADVANTAGE** of this book is that it is the only one available to offer this level of professional advice.

The **BENEFIT** to the sales person who applies this advice is gaining more successful appointments, which in turn improves sales, provides greater financial rewards and increases his/her career status!"

How to make a successful appointment in l0 easy stages
7. USING YOUR SALES SKILLS - OVERCOMING OBJECTIONS

"I am too busy to talk at present." - "Can you send me a brochure?" - "We have lots of people calling us for meetings everyday."

Making appointments is important. You are more likely to complete a sale when face-to-face with the customer. So when someone says, "I am too busy to talk", ask when it would be more convenient to call back.

If they say, "Put something in the mail", reply with, "I can, but I usually meet with people to discuss our business. It helps to explain and answer questions on the spot and takes only about l5 minutes".

A response to, "We have lots of people calling everyday", could be, "I am sure you do, as you are regarded as the best in the business. I've researched your organisation (make sure that you have) and have found some areas where I think we could be of value to you".

When attempting to make telephone appointments, these are three main objections you should be ready for. Overcome these and the rest will be plain sailing.

A word on objection handling for future reference

Many sales training programs devote substantial time in giving their delegates clever responses to overcome any objections made by their customers. But you'll find that most hurdles are actually requests for more information or clarification of relevant points. Price is a consistent enquiry - a natural enough point since we all want to know the exact cost. Most of your customers will know their financial boundaries and will have budget limitations.

So far you have learnt about the importance of research, making the call, establishing needs and arousing interest. By now you will have used some of your sales skills to promote your product. By now an objection should be viewed as less of a negative buying signal.

How to make a successful appointment in 10 easy stages
7. USING YOUR SALES SKILLS - OVERCOMING OBJECTIONS

If you have thoroughly prepared yourself then you should be confident enough to deal with objections. If the same objection reoccurs then look again at the words you've been using. Maybe you could work a little extra into your 'script' and defuse any potential objections before they occur. Many people have their own established buying process and take time checking through information before making a final decision, so it makes sense to go at their pace, answering questions as they are asked.

During our sales training we will assist you in overcoming difficult barriers, objections or recurrent requests for information. We will also give you some new tools to work with....

"You are not a brochure on legs...."

Promote

A lot of time is devoted to product training; it is essential you are familiar with what you are selling in order to talk competently and confidently about it to customers. Learning about anything new takes time, and we each have very different ways of acquiring information. As you have seen from the section on 'Features, Advantages and Benefits', being able to identify your unique selling points ensures you earn business ahead of the competition.

When a potential customer requests details of your product or service, what is it they really want? They could simply be gathering information (research) in the same way as you, so it is wise to establish exactly what information you should send. A corporate brochure will not be read immediately, so attach a letter of introduction with a contact name, and a time for your follow-up call.

On occasions when you are asked to put information in the mail, ask instead if you can arrange a meeting (10-15 minutes) - no hard sell, just a brief get-together to establish exact requirements. If you do send a letter and brochure, make a note in your diary to follow-up

continued

with a call to arrange a meeting. Avoid going into too much detail over the telephone. It can get quite boring for the listener and you may be making the mistake of spraying the customer with too much information. Offer details only when the customer requests it. Keep it simple and remember you are not a brochure on legs!

Listening

Listening is an undervalued skill and an area normally overlooked by sales training programs.

It is an acquired skill and one that needs to be reviewed on a regular basis to be truly effective. The preconception that successful sales people talk more than listen is actually quite wrong. The most successful business people listen far more than they speak. By actively listening to their customers, they can more easily respond to their needs.

If you want to test out the powerful sales tool of listening, try these few tips when in conversation with a friend or partner:

- **Sit comfortably**
- **Keep quiet and attentive throughout**
- **Nod your head to show understanding**
- **Maintain contact with the talker (but do not stare!)**
- **Check you understand by reflecting back what you hear**
- **Avoid evaluating what is being said**
- **Demonstrate interest in the talker**
- **Empathise; try to put yourself in the talker's shoes**
- **Allow any silences without embarrassment**
- **Summarise at the end (business situations)**

How to make a successful appointment in I0 easy stages
8. ASKING FOR APPOINTMENT AND OFFERING ALTERNATIVES

At this stage of your call, providing you have put all that you have learnt so far into practice, you should be in a position to ask for the appointment.

People today are generally very busy, with little diary time to play with. So when arranging a meeting, allow the customer a choice of times that fit in with their work schedule. If you have given an impression that you are also very busy, then remember to ask for an appointment in 2/3 weeks time. Many customers set aside certain days for seeing new suppliers, so try to accommodate their schedule. It is vital, at this stage, that you do not appear inflexible.

Try not to make the customer feel pressurised - you can make them feel uncomfortable if you push for a meeting which conflicts with their busy schedule. The following techniques will focus their attention on making the appointment without frightening them off.

- **Offer either a morning or afternoon meeting at a convenient time.**
- **Offer alternative days, such as Wednesday or Friday.**
- **Say that you already have an appointment in the area on that day.**

That way they will be assured that you don't intend spending too much time with them.

How to make a successful appointment in 10 easy stages
8. ASKING FOR APPOINTMENT AND OFFERING ALTERNATIVES

Many time-management-training courses use these types of techniques. Offering a selection of alternatives shows your flexibility, so do not be put off if settling on mutually agreeable meeting times take a little while. Also, remember to use your own words and don't forget your sense of humour! It's one of the best ways to build rapport.

The appointment venue will depend on the product or service that you are promoting. Most often the initial meeting to provide more details and field questions may take place at the customer's work place. If they need to experience the product or service that you are providing then it will be important that they visit your location.

An afternoon (especially Friday!) is always a good time for the client to visit you - they can get home a little earlier! The easier the agreed venue is to reach, the better the chances of your customer keeping the appointment. Always arrange for an easy-to-understand location map to be sent to them with your letter of confirmation. You can always 'resell' the appointment slot should they change their mind.

"THE MOST OBVIOUS MESSAGE HERE IS TO ACTUALLY ASK FOR THE APPOINTMENT.

If you've handled the conversation correctly it should be a natural progression for you to now meet up face to face!"

How to make a successful appointment in 10 easy stages
9. CLOSING THE CALL

When you have arranged the appointment with the customer, always remember to confirm all the relevant details before finishing the call:

- **Time**
- **Venue with location map**
- **Who will be meeting the customer?**
- **The customer's full name and title**
- **Address to send the confirmation to**
- **Confirm the appointment in writing**

"Reward yourself step by step from a good call to a good day's work and review every positive action as your future success."

"Now, make another call."

How to make a successful appointment in 10 easy stages
10. CONFIRMING APPOINTMENT AND UPDATING RECORDS

● **Your written confirmation**
By either a letter, an e-mail or a compliment slip confirming the meeting, together with a location map. Enclose a brochure or flyer if you have discussed this during the call.

● **Your diary system**
Update your diary system and add the customer's name and telephone number so that it is to hand, rather than in a separate file (which you are only likely to remember to take with you when driving to the meeting!)

● **Your sales records/database**
Update them now using any relevant information from your call that you feel will be helpful. This will later be useful in reminding you what was discussed, particularly if the appointment is a few days or weeks away.

Avoid any embarrassing situations in the future and make doubly sure that all details and names are correct!

"I find that record cards really help with my preparation."

How to make a successful appointment in 10 easy stages
10. CONFIRMING APPOINTMENT AND UPDATING RECORDS

Write down any information you learn about the customer or the organisation during the course of the conversation. You can then read this before the meeting.

RECORD CARD

Customer name _____

Company size _____

Business title _____

Tel _____

Fax _____

E-mail _____

Address _____

_____

NOTES FOR THE BACK OF THE RECORD CARD

11/2 Called and left a message. Called back discussed with buyer (Fred Smith) current needs. Arranged meeting for 21/2. Confirm in writing with details of meeting and venue location, etc. Remember: He's just been promoted to Senior V.P.

21/2 Meeting went well - wants a proposal on XYZ range, follow-up meeting and presentation for 3/3.

Help yourself

TITLES AVAILABLE IN THE LITTLE DEMON SALES SERIES

How to Make Successful Appointments

Your Customers are People - develop consultancy skills

Customer Analysis - maximise sales time

Direct Marketing - how to do it and succeed

Overcoming Sales Aversion - overcome your sales demons

Making Successful Sales Presentations

Making Successful Business Deals - the art of negotiating

High Performance Sales Managers

Recruiting Sales People - exciting new techniques and ideas

Coaching - a success formula

Sales War Stories - a collection of funny sales situations

ORDERING AND FURTHER INFORMATION

To discuss our three distinctive services - training, corporate development and publishing, or to order any of the Little Demon Pocket Books, contact us on:

Freephone +44 0800 358 8003

Fax + 44 (0) 1905 451221

Email: sales@littledemon.com

www. littledemon.com

ONE-DAY TRAINING PROGRAMMES

Details for one-day training on all titles (except War Stories), available on request.